YOUTH
SERVICES

ATLAS OF WORLD FAITHS

BUDDHISM

Anita Ganeri

A+

Smart Apple Media

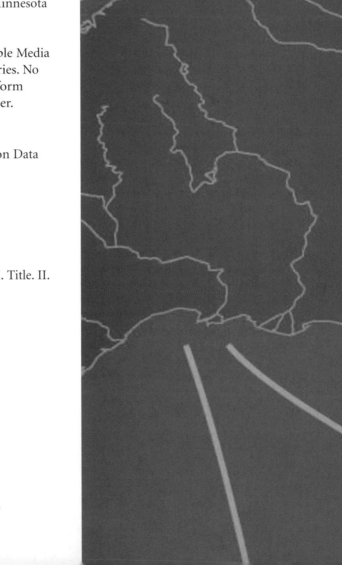

This book has been published in cooperation with
Arcturus Publishing Limited.

Series concept: Alex Woolf
Editor and picture researcher: Alex Woolf
Designer: Simon Borrough
Cartography: Encompass Graphics
Consultant: Douglas G. Heming

Picture credits:
Art Archive: 13 (Musée Guimet Paris/Dagli Orti), 15.
Corbis: 4 (Michael Freeman), 6 (Lindsay Hebberd),
cover and 8 (Blaine Harrington III), 10 (Lindsay
Hebberd), 16 (Lindsay Hebberd), 19 (Christine
Osborne), 20 (Wolfgang Kaehler), 22 (Kevin R Morris),
24 (Pierre Colombel), 27 (Chris Lisle), 28 (Jose Fuste
Raga), 31 (Craig Lovell), 32 (Werner Forman), 34
(Galen Rowell), 36 (Chaiwat Subprasom/Reuters), 39
(Bettmann), 40 (Bojan Brecelj).

Published in the United States by Smart Apple Media
2140 Howard Drive West, North Mankato, Minnesota
56003

Library of Congress Cataloging-in-Publication Data

Ganeri, Anita, 1961–
Buddism / by Anita Ganeri.
p. cm.—(Atlas of world faiths)
Includes index.
ISBN 978-1-59920-058-3
1. Buddhism—History—Juvenile literature. I. Title. II.
Series.

BQ4032.G355 2007
294.309—dc22   2007007621

9 8 7 6 5 4 3 2 1

CONTENTS

This stone carving from Cambodia shows the birth of Siddhartha Gautama, who later became the Buddha, in the garden in Lumbini, Nepal.

One of the world's major religions, Buddhism began in northern India approximately 2,500 years ago when a man named Siddhartha Gautama taught people a new way to live. He became known as the Buddha, or the "Enlightened One," and his teachings were known as the dharma. Since then, Buddhism has spread to countries all over the world, both in its Asian homeland and beyond. In each place, it has adapted to local traditions, merged with local beliefs, and faced many changes and challenges.

Birth of the Buddha The dates usually given for the life of Siddhartha Gautama are 563–483 BCE, although some scholars prefer 448–368 BCE. Legend says that he was the son of King Shuddhodana, the chief of the Shakya clan who lived in northeastern India, on the border with present-day Nepal. During her pregnancy, his mother, Queen Maya, dreamed that she was visited by a white elephant. This was a sign that the child she was carrying was destined to be a great person.

According to tradition, Siddhartha was born on the night of a full moon in May, in a beautiful garden in Lumbini, Nepal. There are many stories to indicate that this was no ordinary birth. The gods showered the baby with flower petals and a rumbling earthquake shook the earth. Seven days later, Queen Maya died, and Siddhartha was raised by his aunt in his father's luxurious palace.

A life of luxury Shortly after Siddhartha was born, a wise man named Asita came to the palace to

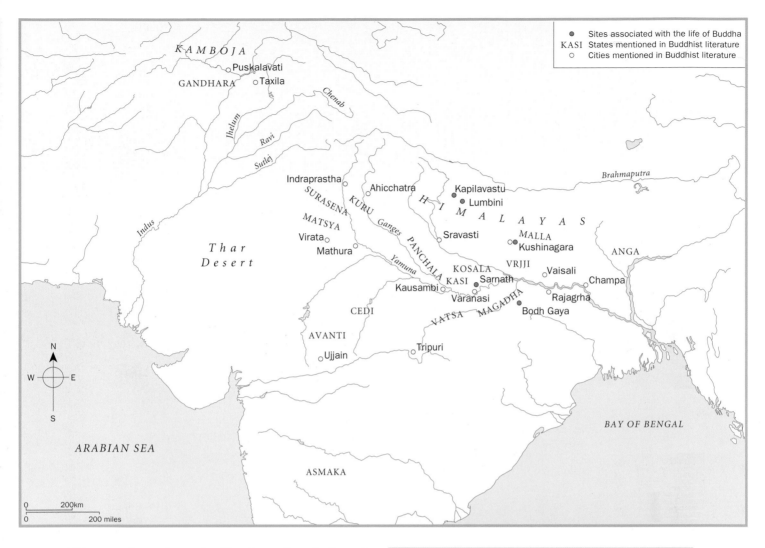

Sites associated with the life of Buddha
KASI States mentioned in Buddhist literature
○ Cities mentioned in Buddhist literature

This map shows the main cities in northern India and Nepal at the time of Siddhartha's birth. Siddhartha grew up in his father's palace in Kapilavastu.

visit the baby. Asita predicted Siddhartha's future. He told the king that his son would grow up to be either a great ruler or a great teacher, depending on what he discovered about suffering in life. Determined that Siddhartha should rule after him, the king tried to keep all knowledge of suffering from his son. He kept Siddhartha safely inside his magnificent palace, sheltered from the outside world and surrounded by the finest things. As part of his education, Siddhartha learned the skills he would need to be a king and a warrior, including archery, fencing, and riding horses. Legend says, when he was 16 years old, he married Yashodhara, a princess from a neighboring kingdom. Following the custom of the time, he won her hand in an archery contest.

RELIGIONS IN INDIA

The period in which Siddhartha was born seems to have been a time of great religious change and upheaval in India. Old ideas were being challenged and debated, and new ideas were being put forward. At that time, the main religion in northwestern India was Hinduism. Siddhartha may have been raised as a Hindu, although no one is sure. When he became the Buddha, he criticized the power of the upper-class Hindu priests and the formal nature of the Hindu religion, which seemed to exclude ordinary people. The Buddha taught that his path was open to everyone—it did not matter if people were rich or poor, what jobs they did, or what part of society they belonged to.

The Mahabodhi Temple in Bodh Gaya, India, where the Buddha gained enlightenment, is topped by a 164-foot-high (50 m), pyramid-shaped spire. A large, gilded image of the Buddha is inside the temple.

The Four Sights For many years, Siddhartha lived in great comfort. Under the king's careful supervision, he led a sheltered life and never saw any kind of suffering. However, when he was 29 years old, he had an experience that changed his life. Disobeying his father's orders, he went for a chariot ride outside the walls of the palace. There he saw an old person, an ill person, and a corpse. He had never seen such suffering before and was deeply shocked. Then he saw a wandering holy man. This man had given up his home

and material possessions but still looked happy and contented.

Search for the truth Siddhartha decided to follow the holy man's example and dedicate his life to searching for a way to end suffering. That night, he secretly left home, cut off his long hair, and exchanged his fine clothes for rags. From then on, he lived as a wandering holy man with no money, belongings, or home. Siddhartha spent some time with two religious teachers, learning how to meditate. Next, he spent six years living in the forest with a group of five holy men. They lived very hard lives, believing that this was the way to wisdom. Siddhartha endured a series of terrible hardships, but they did not help him on his quest.

Enlightenment
Exhausted and weak, Siddhartha left his companions and made his way to the village of Bodh Gaya in northeastern India. One evening, he sat underneath a tall bo, or bodhi, tree to meditate, vowing not to move until he had discovered the truth. According to legend, Siddhartha was visited during the night by Mara, the "evil one," who tried to tempt him away from his search. But nothing that Mara said or did could disturb Siddhartha's concentration, and as the night drew on, he found the answers he had been looking for. Finally, he realized the truth about why people suffered and how he could help them. He had become the Buddha, "the Enlightened One."

GREAT HARDSHIPS

"I took food only once a day, or one in two or seven days. I lived on the roots and fruits of the forest, eating only those that fell of their own accord. I wore coarse clothes and rags from a garbage heap. I became one who always stands and never sits. I made my bed on thorns. The dust and dirt of the years accumulated on my body. Because I ate so little, my limbs became like the knotted joints of withered creepers, my backbone stuck out like a row of beads, and my ribs like the rafters of a tumbledown shed."

From the *Maha-Saccaka Sutra*

This map shows the sites of important events in the Buddha's life. He was born in Lumbini, gained enlightenment in Bodh Gaya, gave his first teaching in Sarnath, and died in Kushinagara.

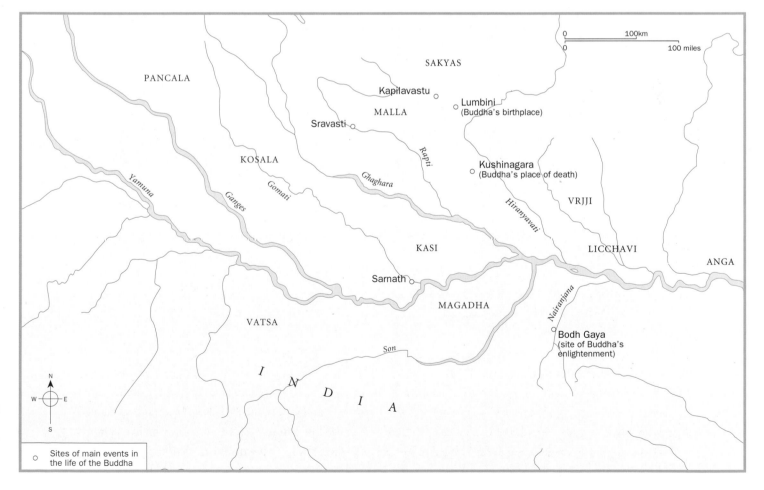

○ Sites of main events in the life of the Buddha

The first teaching

After his enlightenment, the Buddha spent several days reflecting on his experiences and continuing to meditate. He felt a deep sense of peace and joyfulness. During this time, he found his first followers—two passing merchants who brought him food. He then decided to teach his former meditation teachers what he had learned. Discovering they were dead, he thought of the five holy men who had been his companions in the forest. He found them in the deer park in Sarnath, in northern India. He gave his first lesson, explaining to the five holy men the cause of suffering. This teaching is called the Four Noble Truths. The Buddha taught that everyone experiences suffering in life and that this suffering is caused by people not being content with what they have. However, the Buddha teaches there is a way to end suffering by following the Noble Eightfold Path.

THE NOBLE EIGHTFOLD PATH

From his experience, the Buddha knew that neither great luxury nor great hardship led to happiness. He taught a middle path called the Noble Eightfold Path. There are eight parts to the path:

1. Right understanding—understanding the truth of the Buddha's teaching.
2. Right intention—having compassion for other people and thinking about them in a kind and generous way.
3. Right speech—not telling lies, swearing, or speaking unkindly.
4. Right action—not stealing, killing, or performing any actions which might harm or upset other people.
5. Right livelihood—earning a living in a way that does not harm others.
6. Right effort—making an effort to be kind and compassionate.
7. Right mindfulness—being aware of your actions and thoughts.
8. Right concentration—training your mind to be calm and clear.

Many Buddhists have followed in the Buddha's footsteps and become monks like him. This young monk is studying the sacred texts in a monastery.

This map shows early Buddhist settlements in northern India. These were important centers for Buddhist teaching, both by the Buddha himself and the sangha of monks.

Establishing the sangha

The Buddha spent the next 45 years traveling throughout northeastern India and teaching people from all walks of life. Many of his followers dedicated their lives to Buddhism. They became monks and nuns and were known as the sangha. For some Buddhists, the sangha also includes laypersons. During this time, the Buddha helped many other people gain enlightenment. These people became arhats, or "worthy ones," and were sent by the Buddha to teach. Among them was the Buddha's own father. The Buddha's son, Rahula, was ordained as a monk.

The daily life of the Buddha and his monks and nuns is recorded in the Buddhist sacred texts. They possessed only a robe and an alms bowl. In the morning, they arose early and began their daily alms rounds, during which local people gave them food and other gifts. They ate their one meal in the middle of the day. In the afternoons and evenings, they listened to talks by the Buddha or another senior monk, then meditated long into the night. The sangha moved constantly from place to place, except during the rainy season, when they stayed in buildings that became the first monasteries.

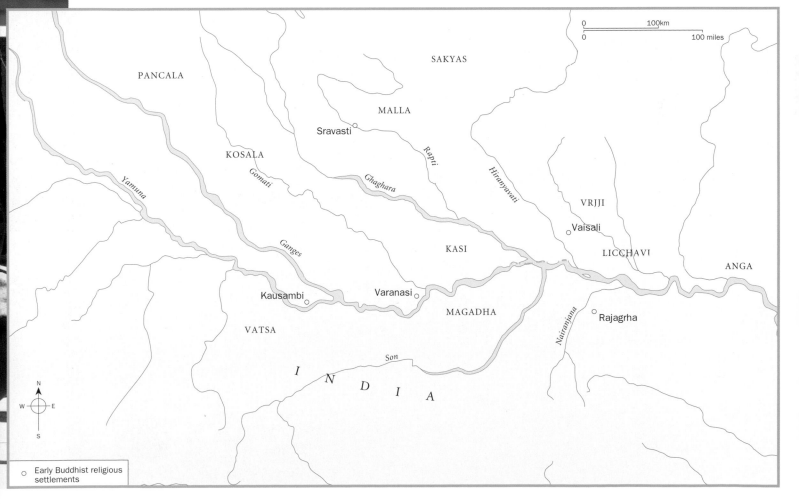

○ Early Buddhist religious settlements

Passing away

At the age of 80, the Buddha became sick with food poisoning and died in a grove of trees near the city of Kushinagara, in northern India. Before he died, he told the monks not to be sad and reminded them that everything changes and passes away. The Buddha did not name a successor but told the monks that his teachings should be their guide. After the Buddha's death, the monks held a six-day ceremony in his honor, and then his body was cremated. His ashes were divided into eight portions and given to eight different rulers. They built dome-shaped monuments, called stupas, over the relics.

The first Buddhist Council

The Buddha's teachings were not written down during his lifetime. Instead, they were memorized by his followers and passed on by word of mouth. According to tradition, shortly after the Buddha's death, a council of 500 monks was called at the village of Rajagrha in northeastern India to agree on the content of the teachings. Two collections of teachings were recited from memory by two of the most senior monks, Upali and Ananda. It is believed that these two collections represented the authentic teachings of the Buddha. However, the collections were still not written down for several centuries.

The second Buddhist Council

About 100 years after the first Buddhist Council, a second council was held in the city of Vesali, in northeastern India. Over the years, differences in Buddhist practice and teaching had begun to emerge. This was not surprising since the sangha was not a single group but was composed of many distinct units with different

According to tradition, the Buddha was lying on his side when he passed away. This is called his *parinirvana*, or passing into nirvana.

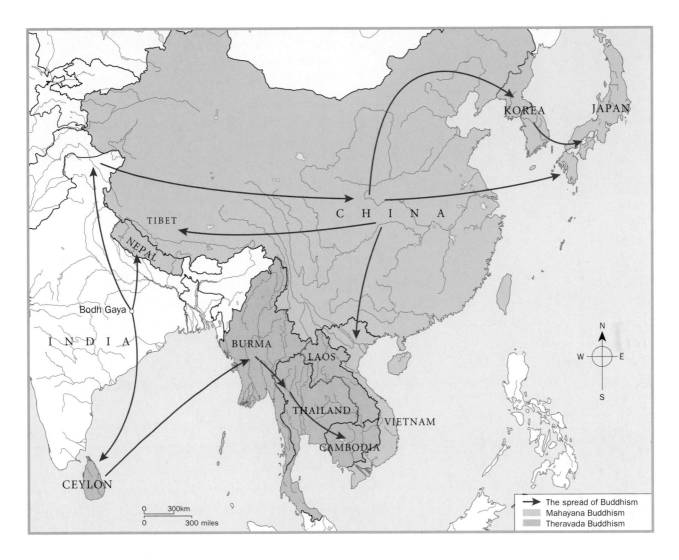

This map shows the spread of Buddhism after the Buddha's death and the countries in which Theravada and Mahayana Buddhism became established.

schools of thought. The main dispute at the second council was about the rules for how monks and nuns should live. Some groups of monks were not strictly following these rules—for example, some were accepting money instead of gifts of food. Eventually, this disagreement led the sangha to split into two groups: the Theravada, "those who follow the way of the elders," and the Mahasanghika, "the great assembly" and the forerunner of the Mahayana.

TWO GREAT SCHOOLS

Theravada Buddhists claim that the pure, unchanged teachings of the Buddha are recorded in their scriptures called the Tripitaka. They believe that the Buddha was a human being, but a very special one. Mahayana Buddhists follow the teachings of the Buddha and other enlightened Buddhist teachers, so they have additional sacred texts. They also worship mythical, godlike figures known as bodhisattvas who choose to help other people overcome suffering. From India, Theravada Buddhism spread south to Ceylon (present-day Sri Lanka), Burma (present-day Myanmar), Laos, Thailand, and Cambodia. Mahayana Buddhism spread north to Tibet, China, Korea, Japan, and Vietnam.

CHAPTER 2:
EARLY BUDDHISM IN INDIA

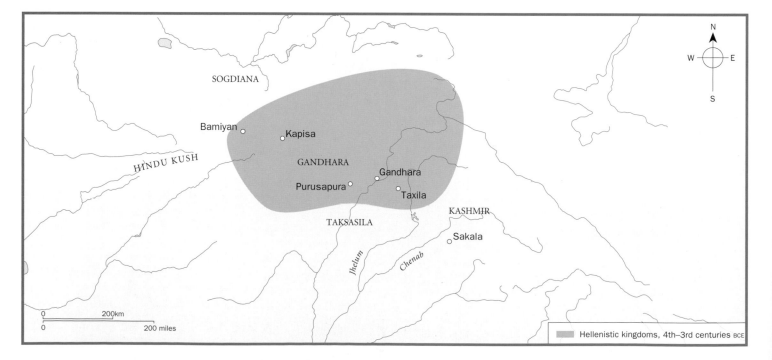

In the centuries after the Buddha's death, Buddhism continued to develop both in India and elsewhere. The Buddha's followers spread his teaching throughout India. Meanwhile, Buddhist missionaries were sent to other Asian countries where they established thriving Buddhist communities. At the same time, many foreign monks came to study at the great Buddhist universities in India. During this period, Buddhism became the main religion in much of India, often with the support of Indian and foreign kings.

The Greeks in India
In 336 BCE, Alexander—later Alexander the Great—ascended the throne of Macedonia in northeastern Greece. Within 13 years, he had conquered a vast empire that stretched from Greece, through Egypt and Persia, and into India. By 330 BCE, Alexander had defeated the Persian emperor Darius. He set out to reach northwestern India, the easternmost part of Darius's empire. Alexander's armies reached India in 326 BCE. At the Battle of the Hydaspes, he defeated the Punjabi king Porus and his troop of 200 war elephants. Alexander was so impressed by Porus's courage that he left him in charge of the Punjab.

SOGDIANA

Bamiyan

Kapisa

HINDU KUSH

GANDHARA

Gandhara

Purusapura

Taxila

KASHMIR

TAKSASILA

Sakala

Jhelum

Chenab

0 — 200km
0 — 200 miles

Hellenistic kingdoms, 4th–3rd centuries BCE

This map shows the location of the Hellenistic (Greek) kingdoms in India during the fourth and third centuries BCE, including the kingdom of Gandhara.

The kingdom of Gandhara

After Alexander's death, a Hellenistic, or Greek, kingdom was established in the area around Gandhara, Purusapura, and Taxila (see map on page 12). The kingdom became known as Gandhara. Buddhist missionaries were soon at work in the region, eventually gaining the support of local rulers such as King Milinda. Gandhara reached its height from the first to the fifth centuries CE under the Buddhist Kushan kings (see page 16). It also became the location of the first great Buddhist university, attracting Buddhist scholars from far and wide. This university, in the city of Taxila, became a starting point for Buddhist missionaries traveling into central Asia. Gandhara survived until the eleventh century, when it was conquered by Muslim invaders.

Images of the Buddha

The first images of the Buddha were produced by Gandharan craftsmen from around the first century. Before this, the Buddha had only been depicted using symbols such as an empty throne, a stupa, a bo tree, a footprint, or an animal. The style of these early images was strongly influenced by Greek art. In Gandharan art, Indian and Greek sculpture combined to produce graceful statues draped in long, flowing robes. From India, traders passing through Gandhara carried Gandharan art into central Asia and China.

This standing Buddha from Gandhara shows the mixture of Indian and Greek styles.

MILINDA'S QUESTIONS

Many of the Greek rulers were influenced by Buddhism, including King Milinda (ruled 155–130 BCE). *Milinda* is the Indian version of the name, Menander. Milinda is said to have had a famous debate about Buddhism with the great teacher and monk, Nagasena. The king asked Nagasena a series of questions about the Buddha's teachings. Milinda was so impressed with Nagasena's answers that he converted to Buddhism. The debate is recorded in an important Buddhist text called *The Questions of King Milinda.*

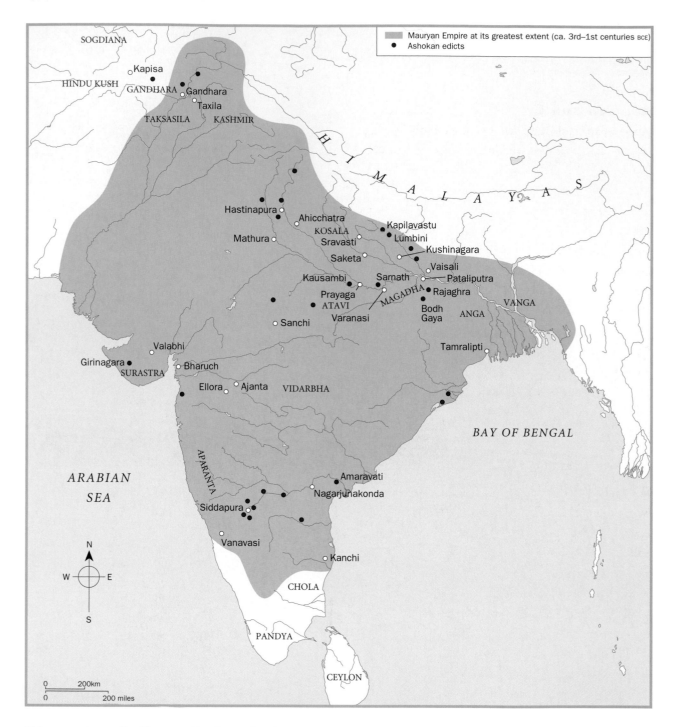

This map shows the Mauryan Empire under Ashoka.

The Mauryan Empire

Around 321 BCE, Chandragupta conquered the area of northern India, where the Buddha had taught, and established the great Mauryan Empire. Chandragupta established his capital at Pataliputra, the modern-day city of Patna. Under the rule of his grandson Ashoka (ruled 265–232 BCE), the empire reached its greatest extent. Soon, most of India, except the extreme south, was under Mauryan rule, but at the cost of thousands of lives. In about 260 BCE, Ashoka launched a particularly ruthless campaign against the region of Kalinga on the eastern coast. It was one of the few places in India that resisted the Mauryans. According to some accounts, 100,000 people were killed in the battle and thousands more were injured or imprisoned. Later, Ashoka was filled with remorse. To make amends, he converted to Buddhism and its teaching of nonviolence.

Ashoka and Buddhism

Ashoka became the greatest patron of Buddhism in ancient India. During his rule, all the existing Buddhist centers were greatly expanded and new monasteries and stupas were built. More importantly, Ashoka vowed to establish a society, not based on war and violence, but on the Buddhist principles of compassion and peace. He also tried to set an example. He traveled throughout the empire, listening to people's opinions about what would make their lives easier. In response, he built wells and reservoirs, established free hospitals for the poor, planted trees, and provided welfare services for prisoners. He gave up hunting, his favorite sport, and instead, went on pilgrimages to holy places associated with the Buddha's life. He also sent missionaries out of India to spread the Buddha's teachings.

Ashoka's edicts

Throughout his empire, Ashoka displayed a series of edicts, carved onto rock faces and sandstone pillars. These proclamations were written in the ancient Indian language of Magadhi and were deciphered for the first time in 1837 by the British scholar James Prinsep. The edicts were located at the borders of the empire and in places connected with the Buddha. Some edicts told of Ashoka's conversion to Buddhism. Others explained the Buddha's teachings and told people to behave accordingly, by living responsible and moral lives, helping others, being generous and truthful, and not killing or harming living beings. Special officers were also appointed to travel throughout the empire and explain the Buddha's teachings.

LION CAPITAL

The famous lion capital once stood on top of one of Ashoka's finest pillars. It was located in the deer park at Sarnath where the Buddha gave his first talk. The four lions face in four different directions to show that the Buddha's teachings reach all four corners of the earth. Below are four royal animals—the horse, bull, lion, and elephant—and four wheels that represent the Buddha's teachings. The lions orginally supported a huge wheel, a symbol of Buddhism. Today, the lion capital is the state symbol of modern India.

Ashoka's lion capital is now in the museum at Sarnath.

The Kushan Empire After Ashoka's death in 231 BCE, the Mauryan Empire began to break up and finally collapsed in 184 BCE. After a period of unrest, India was invaded by the Scythian people from central Asia, who founded the Kushan Empire. Their king, Kanishka (78–102 CE), was an enthusiastic supporter of Buddhism. Around 100 CE, he called Buddhists together for a fourth council in Kashmir. Since the collapse of the Mauryan Empire, Buddhism had split into 18 different groups, or schools. The goal of the fourth council was to bring these different schools together and approve a new set of scriptures, written in Sanskrit, the ancient religious language of India. These scriptures became associated with the Mahayana school.

The rise of the Guptas With the decline of the Kushan Empire, Chandra Gupta I (ruled 319–ca. 335 CE) established the Gupta Empire across northern India. Under the Guptas, a golden age of Indian culture and history began. Literature, art, and religion flourished, and even though the Guptas largely followed the Hindu religion, Buddhism was still given royal support. Great Buddhist universities were established at Nalanda and other locations. New Buddhist texts were written, and many fine works of art were created—including the paintings inside the Buddhist cave temples at Ajanta in western India, which can still be seen today. The Gupta Empire lasted until the sixth century when it was attacked by the Huns from central Asia.

Buddhism declines The Huns destroyed many Buddhist centers in northwestern India, including Taxila. Over the next few centuries, Buddhism survived but no longer had royal support. However, from the

NALANDA UNIVERSITY

The greatest university in the Buddhist world was at Nalanda (modern-day Bihar). At its peak during the fifth century, the university attracted over 10,000 students and 1,500 teachers from all over India and Asia. Subjects included the study of the Buddhist scriptures, Hinduism, philosophy, astronomy, mathematics, and medicine. Among Nalanda's most famous teachers was the monk Nagarjuna, who founded the influential Madhyamika, or "Middle Path," a school of Mahayana Buddhism. His main teaching was on the Buddhist concept of sunyata—emptiness—the idea that nothing has an individual soul or self.

The ruins of the great Buddhist university of Nalanda in Bihar, India.

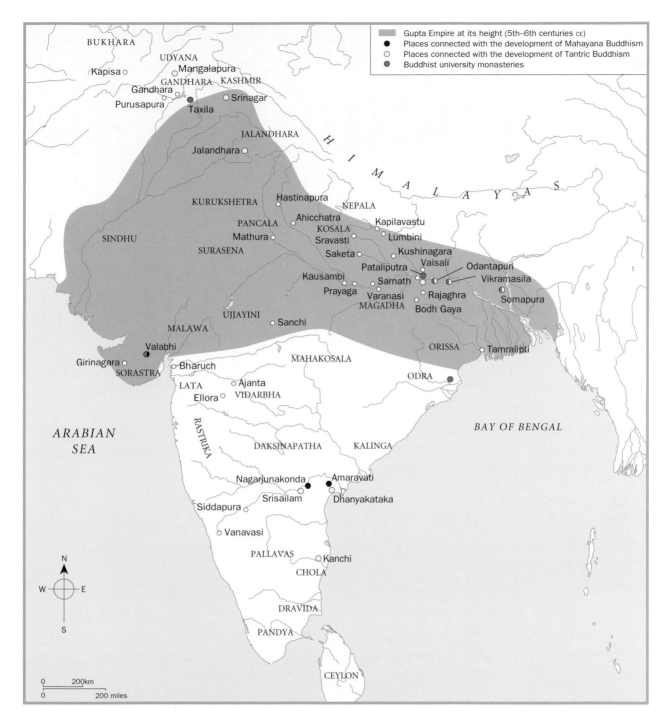

Gupta Empire at its height (5th–6th centuries CE)
● Places connected with the development of Mahayana Buddhism
○ Places connected with the development of Tantric Buddhism
● Buddhist university monasteries

This map shows the location of key Buddhist sites in the Gupta Empire.

eleventh century on, a series of devastating raids by Muslims from Afghanistan finally ended 1,700 years of Buddhism in India. The pacifist nature of Buddhism made it an easy target for the Muslim armies. Monasteries were destroyed, and in 1199, Nalanda was burned to the ground and its monks were slaughtered. Since then, Buddhism has never regained its importance in India, and Hinduism has become the country's major religion. India still attracts Buddhist pilgrims from all over the world to visit its sacred sites, but as recently as 1991, only one percent of Indians considered themselves Buddhists. (See the panel on page 36 for more about modern Buddhism in India.)

CHAPTER 3:
BUDDHISM IN CEYLON AND SOUTHEAST ASIA

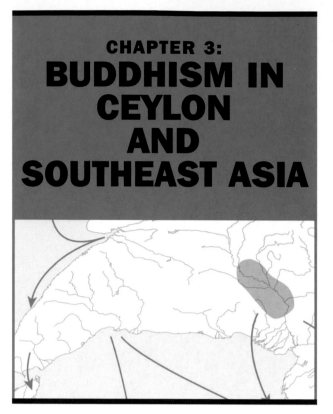

Ashoka's reign was a crucial time for the expansion of Buddhism. From India, Ashoka sent missionary monks to spread the Buddha's teachings. The first country outside India to receive Buddhism was the island of Ceylon (present-day Sri Lanka), off the southern coast of India. Buddhism quickly became Ceylon's major religion and later spread throughout Southeast Asia, including Indonesia, Burma, Vietnam, Cambodia, Laos, and Thailand.

Buddhism reaches Ceylon
Around 250 BCE, Buddhism was introduced in Ceylon by Ashoka's missionaries. They were supposedly led by Ashoka's son, Mahinda, who had become a Buddhist monk. He converted King Tissa to Buddhism. Later, Ashoka's daughter, the nun Sanghamitta, visited the island and brought a cutting of the original bo tree, under which the Buddha gained enlightenment. It was planted in the capital city of Anuradhapura, where it still grows today.

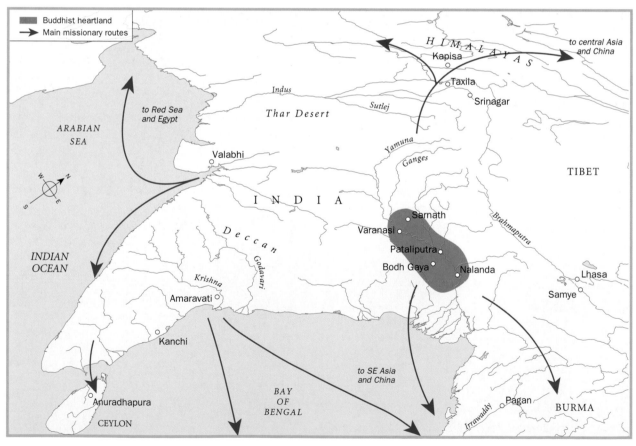

This map shows the main routes taken by the first Buddhist missionaries outside India.

During the second century BCE, Tamil invaders from India ruled parts of Ceylon and Buddhism suffered. Many monks fled or died. Around this time, the Tripitaka was written down out of fear that it would be lost, because there were not enough monks to remember it.

RIVAL MONASTERIES

At Anuradhapura, King Tissa built the Mahavihara (Great Monastery) for Mahinda and his monks. The Mahavihara became the headquarters of Theravada Buddhism. However, in the first century BCE, the monks' position was threatened when another great monastery, the Abhayagiri, was built. The Abhayagiri became associated with Mahayana Buddhism, and a fierce rivalry began between the two monasteries. Mahayana Buddhism did not achieve a lasting hold in Ceylon and, by the twelfth century, the Abhayagiri had declined. This region became, and remains today, a Theravada country.

Buddhism falls and rises

Between the first and seventh centuries CE, Buddhism thrived in Ceylon. However, from the seventh to twelfth centuries, southern Indian kings invaded the island, and Buddhism declined. In 1070, King Vijayabahu (ruled 1055–1110) recaptured the island and began restoring Buddhism. But Ceylon was in such a poor state that the king had to bring an order of monks from Burma to form a new sangha. In the twelfth century, King Parakramabahu (ruled 1153–86) defeated the Indians and built many magnificent monasteries and stupas in the new capital of Polonnaruwa. With the arrival of Europeans on the island in the sixteenth and seventeenth centuries, Buddhism declined as the Europeans tried to convert the Ceylonese to Christianity. There was another Buddhist revival in the eighteenth century when several new orders of monks were formed. From 1796 to 1948, Ceylon was part of the British Empire, attracting followers who helped spread Buddhism to the West.

Buddhism today

After more than 2,300 years, Ceylon—now known as Sri Lanka—remains a proudly Buddhist country and the homeland of the Theravada tradition. Approximately 70 percent of the island's population is Buddhist. With about 15,000 monks, the sangha remains at the center of Buddhist life, and the monks are greatly respected by the community.

A Buddhist shrine at Mihintale, Sri Lanka, where Mahinda met the island's king.

An image of the seated Buddha next to a stupa on the upper terrace at Borobudur. The monument has more than 400 Buddha images.

Buddhism in Indonesia According to tradition, the first Buddhists to reach Southeast Asia were missionaries sent by Ashoka in the third century BCE. They traveled along sea trade routes to the "Land of Gold," which was probably the western coast of Indonesia. But Buddhism really began to make an impact in Indonesia in the first century CE, when many Indians had settled in the region.

Buddhist kingdoms Between approximately 600 and 800 CE, the mainly Buddhist kingdom of Srivijaya ruled Sumatra. By the seventh century, there were Theravada communities in Srivijaya, with Mahayana arriving shortly after. Atisha, the great Indian Buddhist teacher, studied in Srivijaya in the eleventh century, and students traveled from Indonesia to study at Nalanda University. Indonesia was also a regular stopping point for Buddhist monks from China traveling to India.

In Java, both Buddhism and Hinduism were followed, with Buddhism becoming the dominant religion. In the eighth century, the Shailendra kings came to power and were strong patrons of Mahayana Buddhism. Their capital at Palembang became a great center of Buddhist learning. Around 800 CE, the Shailendras sponsored the building of Borobudur.

BOROBUDUR

The astonishing Buddhist monument of Borobudur was built on a hill, in the form of a gigantic stepped pyramid, six stories tall. A stupa stands on the summit. Below this are three circular terraces representing the stages toward enlightenment in a person's life. The entire monument is shaped like a lotus flower, a sacred symbol of Buddhism. Each terrace is decorated with images of the Buddha and with scenes from his life. When Buddhism declined in Indonesia, Borobudur was abandoned. It was rediscovered in 1814.

Buddhism in Burma

Buddhism did not become well established in Burma (present-day Myanmar) until the Mon period, from the fifth to the tenth centuries CE. The Mon people of southern Burma followed the Theravada tradition, as did the Pyu people of central Burma. Mahayana Buddhism may have arrived earlier than Theravada, but it did not become popular. In the eleventh century, King Anuruddha (1044–77) overthrew the Mon and unified the country. During his rule, Theravada Buddhism became firmly established. Anuruddha built his capital at Pagan, which is still famous for its amazing Buddhist ruins. Burma was later invaded by the Thais, who adopted Theravada

Buddhism. In 1886, the country became part of the British Empire. For many people in Burma, Buddhism became a powerful symbol of national identity during this colonial period.

Buddhism today

Beginning in the thirteenth century, Islam became the major religion of Indonesia, although a mixture of Buddhism and Hinduism still survives in Bali and in parts of Java. In the twentieth century, Buddhism enjoyed a revival, and there are now about three million Buddhists in Indonesia.

In Burma—now called Myanmar—Buddhism remains the national religion, practiced by about 85 percent of the population. Despite the country's harsh military government, Buddhism continues to thrive, with thousands of monks and nuns and approximately 6,000 monasteries.

This map shows the spread of Theravada and Mahayana Buddhism into Southeast Asia from the first century BCE.

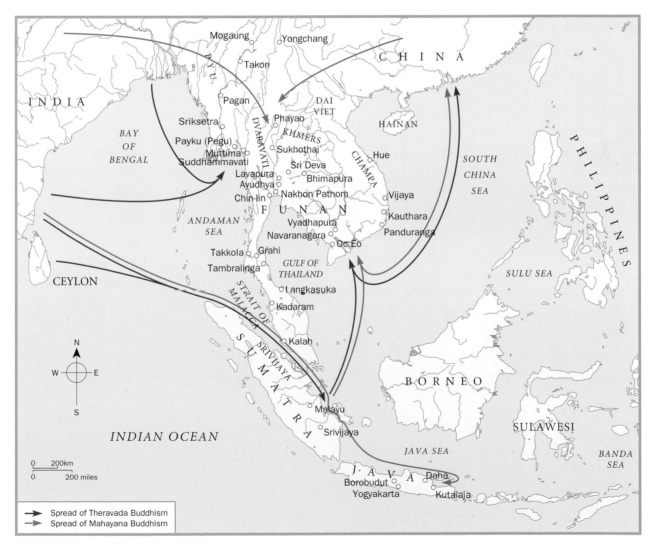

A young monk in Thailand collects alms from a Thai Buddhist outside a monastery. Buddhism remains very strong in Thailand.

Buddhism in Vietnam Theravada missionaries may have reached Vietnam by sea as early as the second century, but the story of Buddhism in Vietnam really begins in 580 CE. Vinitaruci, an Indian monk who had studied in China, arrived in Vietnam and brought Mahayana Buddhism with him. Mahayana was quickly accepted in Vietnam, and when the country was unified in 939, it became the national religion. Two schools of Chinese Mahayana Buddhism—Chan, or Zen, and Pure Land—became popular. Buddhism was well supported by the Vietnamese kings, who regularly appointed monks to key positions at court. Through the following centuries, Buddhism became closely linked with Vietnamese nationalism. From 1883 to 1954, Vietnam came under French rule. Two Buddhist movements played a part in the struggle for independence: the Central Vietnamese Buddhist Association and the General Association of Buddhism in Vietnam.

Buddhism in Cambodia and Laos

In the ninth century, Cambodia had strong links with both India and China, but its Khmer rulers preferred Hinduism to Buddhism. Influenced by the Shailendra kings of Java, the Cambodian kings began to build "temple mountains" like Borobudur, the greatest of which was called Angkor Wat. But unlike the Buddhist Borobudur, the Cambodian monuments were Hindu. This changed during the reign of King Jayavarman VII (ruled 1181–ca. 1215). He converted to Mahayana Buddhism, and the country became Buddhist. Beginning in the early thirteenth century, Cambodia experienced a series of invasions by Thailand. Possibly because of the influence of the Thai invaders, the kings of Cambodia became Theravada Buddhists.

During this time, the neighboring country of Laos fell under the control of the Khmer, the Thais, and Burma. When Laos regained its independence in 1350, Theravada Buddhism was introduced, and the king invited monks from Cambodia and Ceylon to his court to act as his advisors.

Buddhism in Thailand   The Thai kingdom of Sukhothai, which lasted from the early twelfth century to 1350, adopted Theravada Buddhism from the

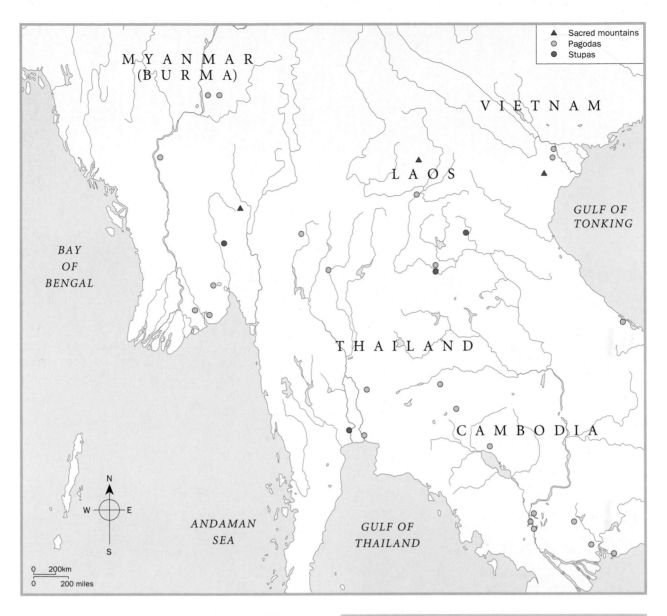

This map shows the location of sacred Buddhist sites in Southeast Asia.

people of Burma. However, it was not until the founding of the kingdom of Ayutthaya in 1350 that Buddhism became the state religion, with the king as head of the sangha. Succeeding kings continued to protect, support, and reform Buddhism. King Rama IV (ruled 1851–68) served for 25 years as a monk before coming to the throne. He revised the sacred texts and founded a new order of monks. Under King Rama V (ruled 1868–1910), these policies continued and the three "Sangha Acts" were passed to define the duties of monks, particularly in the areas of healthcare and education.

MODERN THAI BUDDHISM

The close ties between the Thai king and the Buddhist sangha continue today. The king no longer has as much power, but he is still the honorary head of the sangha. Meanwhile, the government supervises the organization of the sangha. Buddhism remains very strong in Thailand, even as the country becomes more Westernized. Around 94 percent of the population is Buddhist. Many Thai men spend time in the sangha as part of their education. This has helped strengthen the relationship betweeen lay Buddhists and the sangha.

Buddhism reached China around the first century BCE and was probably spread by merchants traveling from India through central Asia along the great trade route known as the Silk Road. By the sixth century, Mahayana Buddhism had become one of China's main religions. From China, Buddhism spread to Korea, and from there to Japan.

These stone sculptures are from the Longmen Caves, one of the most important Buddhist sites in China.

The arrival of Buddhism

When Buddhism first arrived in China, it was not a great success. The Chinese already had their own religious traditions—predominantly Confucianism and Taoism—and thought that these were superior to Buddhism. Despite this, some Buddhist texts were translated into Chinese, and Chinese people began to join the sangha. By the fourth century, there were 24,000 Buddhist monks and almost 2,000 monasteries in China. Buddhism did not replace the Chinese religions but developed alongside them. The sixth to the ninth centuries were a golden age for Chinese Buddhism. Taoism remained popular with the aristocracy, but Buddhism appealed to ordinary people. During this period, many different schools of Chinese Mahayana Buddhism developed. In the ninth century, a backlash began against the power and wealth of the Buddhist monasteries. Buddhism survived but was greatly weakened. In the twelfth century, it lost support to Confucianism, which became the official state religion.

PILGRIM MONKS

To collect Buddhist texts for translation into Chinese, several Chinese monks made long, grueling journeys to India. Faxian (338–422 CE) began his journey in 399. He finally reached India after crossing the deadly Taklimakan Desert and the Pamir Mountains, which were said to shelter dragons that spewed poison. More than 200 years later, another monk, Xuanzang (602–664 CE) followed in Faxian's footsteps. Xuanzang visited many Buddhist sites in India, including Nalanda University, and brought back so many texts that he needed 20 horses to carry them all.

Chinese Buddhist schools

Two of the most popular schools of Chinese Buddhism were Ching t'u (Pure Land) and Chan (Zen, in Japanese). Pure Land is based on the worship of the Buddha Amitabha, who is believed to live in a heavenly land called the "Pure Land." If people have faith in Amitabha and chant his name, they will be reborn in the Pure Land. From there, they will be able to progress easily toward enlightenment.

Tradition says that Chan was brought to China by the Indian monk Bodhidharma in the early sixth century. Chan is a type of Buddhism based on meditation as a way of experiencing reality and seeing the world as it really is. Many different meditation techniques are used. One method is to sit quietly for long periods, with no thoughts or wishes, staring at a wall.

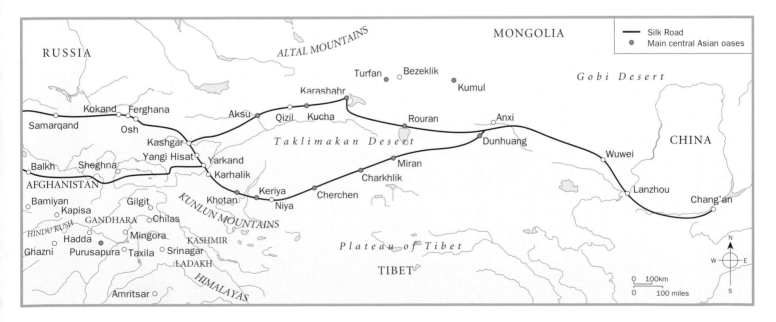

The Silk Road crossed central Asia, linking China with India and the West.

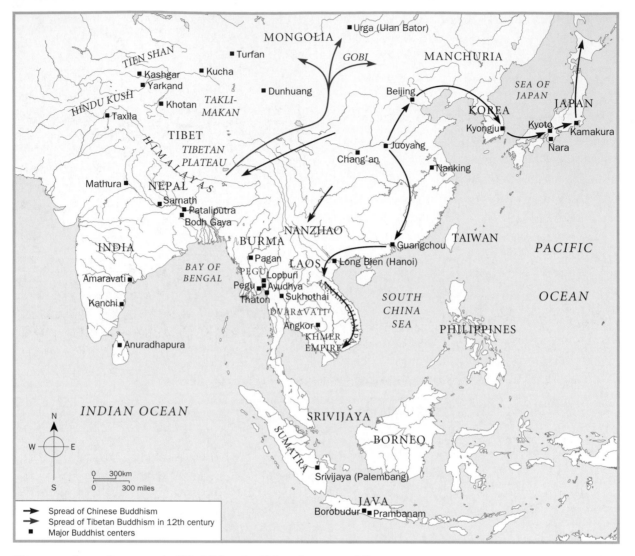

This map shows the spread of Buddhism to China, Japan, and Korea.

Decline of Chinese Buddhism In
1949, China came under Communist rule. The
Communists harshly suppressed Buddhism and other
religions. This persecution was particularly brutal
during the Cultural Revolution (1966–69), when
Buddhism was practically wiped out. In the 1980s, some
Buddhist temples were rebuilt and Buddhist
organizations revived. However, this revival was halted
in the late 1980s when the Communist government
again cracked down on Buddhism.

Buddhism reaches Korea Even though
Buddhism declined in China, Chinese Buddhism had a
major influence on the rest of the region. Buddhism
may have reached Korea in the fourth century, when

Chinese monks visited Korea, bringing Buddhist texts
and images and building several monasteries. Buddhism
flourished during the Silla Dynasty (618–935 CE), when
it received royal support. Silla monks traveled to China
and India to bring back the latest teachings. Buddhism
remained the state religion until the fourteenth century.

The first ruler of the Koryo dynasty (918–1392) was
King T'aejo, a devout Buddhist who built 10 great
monasteries in his capital. Senior monks were appointed
as royal advisors, and it was typical for members of the
royal family to become monks. A new edition of the
Korean scriptures, with more than 5,000 volumes, was
collected and printed. Under the Koryos, the
monasteries became rich and powerful.

Monastic powers were greatly reduced during the Choson dynasty (1392–1910), when stricter rules were imposed on the monks. Nonetheless, Buddhism continued to enjoy royal support for many years.

Modern Korean Buddhism

From 1910 to 1945, Korea came under Japanese control. Monasteries were divided up and there were conflicts between different groups of monks. During these years, the monk Han Yongun (1879–1944) campaigned hard to protect Korean Buddhism. After World War II (1939–45), the country was divided into North and South Korea. The northern Communist government suppressed religion, and Buddhism was almost wiped out. In the south, Buddhism is still widely followed. Many "new religions" have been established in South Korea, most of which are other forms of Buddhism.

CHINUL AND CHOGYE

One of the most important Korean Buddhists was the monk Chinul (1158–1210). He became a Son, or Chan, monk when he was seven years old. Chinul passed all his monastic examinations, but instead of rising to a high position in the sangha, he decided to form his own Buddhist school. It was called the Chogye school and attracted many followers, including the king. When Chinul opened his Suson Monastery in 1205, the king declared 120 days of national celebrations. Chogye remains the main Buddhist school, and the Suson Monastery continues to be a major center of Korean Buddhism.

Colorful lanterns are hung outside the Pulguk-sa Buddhist Temple in Kyongu, Korea.

BUDDHISM

Buddhism in Japan Mahayana Buddhism came to Japan from Korea in the sixth century CE. A Korean king sent a mission to the Japanese emperor that included Buddhist monks carrying texts and images of the Buddha. Under Prince Shotoku (ruled 574–622 CE), Buddhism flourished in Japan, existing alongside Shinto, the ancient Japanese religion. Shotoku built Buddhist temples and monasteries and made Buddhism the state religion. In the eighth century, two forms of Chinese Buddhism—Tendai and Shingon—became popular. Both had mountain-top monasteries as their headquarters in Japan. In the twelfth and thirteenth centuries, new schools developed, including Zen. Zen monasteries played an important role in protecting the teachings of Buddhism during the turbulent fourteenth and fifteenth centuries, when many wars were fought between rival warlords. In the sixteenth and seventeenth centuries, Christian missionaries arrived in Japan. To preserve Buddhism, the emperor ordered all Japanese people, religious or not, to register with a Buddhist monastery.

A great teacher One of the greatest teachers of Japanese Buddhism was the monk Nichiren (1222–82). He studied at the great Tendai monastery on Mount Hiei outside Kyoto but left to form his own school of Buddhism. He simplified the Tendai teachings to focus on the Lotus Sutra and taught his followers that they could purify their minds by chanting the name of the Lotus Sutra. Nichiren was frequently persecuted because of his outspoken attacks on other Buddhist groups. He escaped execution but was banished to a remote island. Despite this, Nichiren's influence remains strong today, and several modern Japanese Buddhist groups follow his teachings.

The great Buddha statue at Kamakura, Japan, dates from the thirteenth century.

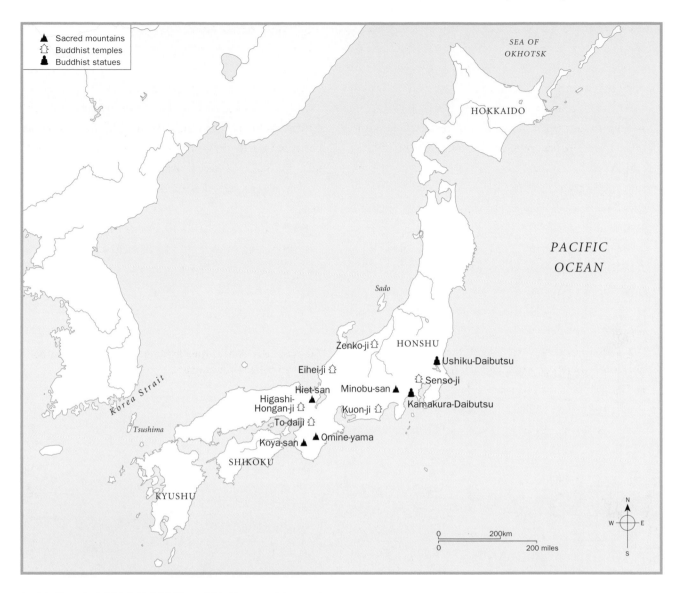

- ▲ Sacred mountains
- ⛩ Buddhist temples
- ▲ Buddhist statues

SEA OF OKHOTSK

HOKKAIDO

PACIFIC OCEAN

Sado

Zenko-ji ⛩

HONSHU

▲ Ushiku-Daibutsu

Eihei-ji ⛩

⛩ Senso-ji

Hiet-san ▲   Minobu-san ▲

Higashi-
Hongan-ji ▲

Kuon-ji ⛩   Kamakura-Daibutsu

To-daiji ⛩

Koya-san ▲   ▲ Omine-yama

SHIKOKU

Korea Strait

Tsushima

KYUSHU

0   200km
0   200 miles

N
W   E
S

This map shows sacred Buddhist sites in Japan, including mountains, temples, and statues.

THE LOTUS SUTRA

The Lotus Sutra is one of the most important and popular Mahayana Buddhist texts. It is treated with great honor and respect. A long collection of stories and verses, it takes the form of a speech given by the Buddha to a huge audience of followers and bodhisattvas. One of its key teachings is that everyone, not only holy men and women, can achieve enlightenment. To illustrate this, the Buddha compared himself to a raincloud that pours equally on every plant. In the same way, the Buddha's teachings are available to everyone.

Modern Japanese Buddhism

In the nineteenth century, Shinto became the state religion of Japan and remained so until the end of World War II. But Buddhism continued to thrive. Today, about 75 percent of Japanese people consider themselves Buddhists. Many actually follow a mixture of Buddhism and Shinto, and in many places, Buddhist temples and Shinto shrines stand side by side. Also, new religious groups have developed based on ancient Buddhist teachings. These include Soka-gakkai, which is a form of Nichiren Buddhism.

CHAPTER 5: BUDDHISM IN TIBET

Tibet remained a Buddhist country with thriving monasteries and thousands of monks. Today, under Chinese rule, Buddhism faces an uncertain future.

Early Tibetan Buddhism The story of Buddhism in Tibet begins with King Songtsen Gampo (ruled ca. 609–50 CE). Two of his wives, a Nepalese princess and a Chinese princess, were devout Buddhists. It is unclear whether the king himself converted to Buddhism, but he built two magnificent Buddhist temples, the Jokhang and the Rampoche, for his wives. These housed two statues of the Buddha that the wives had brought with them as dowries. Later, King Khrisong Detsen (ruled 755–97) made Buddhism the state religion with the help of great Indian teachers, including Padmasambhava. This did not occur without

Contact with India during the seventh century led to the introduction of Buddhism in Tibet. A long struggle followed between Buddhism and the local religion, Bon. However, by the fourteenth century, Buddhism had become the state religion. For centuries,

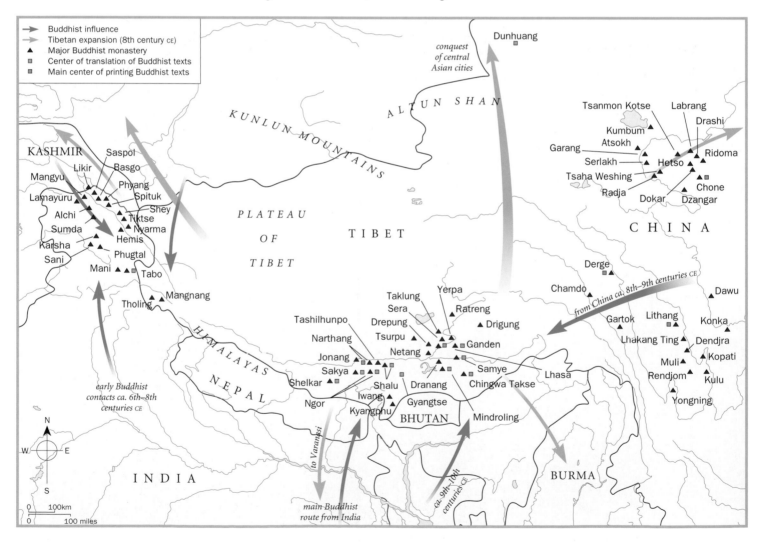

This map shows the growth of Buddhism in Tibet and other major Buddhist centers.

opposition, and a long struggle began between Buddhism and Bon, the established religion of Tibet. During his rule, from 817–36 CE, King Ralpachan went so far as to become a Buddhist monk. He was assassinated by his brother, Langdarma, a strong supporter of Bon. Langdarma persecuted the Buddhists, destroying monasteries and killing many monks. However, in 842 CE, he was killed by a Buddhist monk. In the tenth and eleventh centuries, many monks fled to Tibet from India to escape the Muslim attacks. As a result, Tibetan Buddhism revived and flourished.

Translating texts

King Songtsen Gampo sent a translator to India to create an alphabet for the Tibetan language, which had not yet been written down. This enabled Buddhist sacred texts from India to be translated from Sanskrit into Tibetan. By the eighth century, Tibetan translators were hard at work, and over several centuries, they created a huge collection of holy books. Tibetan texts belong to two main groups—the Kanjur and the Tenjur. The Kanjur has 108 volumes and contains the words of the Buddha. The Tenjur has 360 volumes and contains commentaries on the Kanjur texts. This work also helped preserve the original Indian texts, as Buddhism declined in India.

LOTUS BORN

The famous Indian teacher, Padmasambhava, arrived in Tibet in the late eighth century. He helped establish Buddhism among the ordinary Tibetan people. Padmasambhava's name means "lotus born;" legend says he was born from a lotus flower. He was considered a great saint with amazing magical powers. According to tradition, King Khrisong Detsen organized a magic contest between Padmasambhava and the most powerful Bon priests and their demon allies. Padmasambhava is said to have used spectacular magic to overcome the priests and demons and convert them to Buddhism. During Padmasambhava's time, the first Buddhist monastery was built at Samye, and the first Tibetans became monks.

A Tibetan Buddhist monk reads the sacred texts.

Tibetan Buddhism

Tibetan Buddhism A unique form of Buddhism is practiced in Tibet, known as tantric Buddhism. Tantric Buddhism is a type of Mahayana Buddhism that uses magic spells and rituals to help people gain enlightenment. It gets its name from a collection of mysterious sacred texts called the Tantras and was introduced in Tibet by Padmasambhava. Tibetan Buddhism is sometimes called Vajrayana, which means "thunderbolt" in Sanskrit. This is because it is seen as a swift path to enlightenment, as fast as a speeding thunderbolt.

An image of the bodhisattva, Avalokitesvara. Tibetans believe that the Dalai Lama is Avalokitesvara in human form.

MARPA AND MILAREPA

The Kagyupa group within Tibetan Buddhism was founded by a great Buddhist teacher named Marpa (1012–96). His disciple Milarepa (1040–1123) became one of Tibet's most revered saints. Legend says Milarepa turned to Buddhism to make amends for using magic to punish his uncle. After his training with Marpa, Milarepa spent most of his life living in a lonely mountain cave. He dressed in rags and ate boiled nettles. Despite his harsh existence, Milarepa is famous for his collection of songs and poems that describe the joy of enlightenment. Known as *The Hundred Thousand Songs of Milarepa*, this remains one of the most popular sacred texts of Tibetan Buddhism.

Different schools In the ninth century, several different schools of Tibetan Buddhism began to develop. The oldest is the Nyingmapa group, which traces its teachings back to Padmasambhava. He is thought to have buried a collection of sacred texts in the mountains that would be found when people were ready for the teachings. The Kadampa group was founded by another Indian monk, Atisha (982–1054). It stressed discipline and morality and had strict rules for its monks. Another group, the Sakyapas, were named after the gray color of the earth around their monastery. They became very powerful in the twelfth and thirteenth centuries.

The rise of the Gelukpas By the

thirteenth century, Buddhism was flourishing in Tibet. Several of the Buddhist groups became involved in politics. In 1240, the Mongols from the northwest threatened to invade Tibet. To protect Tibet, the head of the Sakyapas, Sakya Pandita (1182–1251), traveled to the Mongol court. He offered to become spiritual advisor to the Mongol leader in return for the Mongols leaving Tibet in peace. The plan worked, and the Sakyapas became the rulers of Tibet.

By the early fifteenth century, power passed to another group. The Gelukpas were founded in 1409 by the Tibetan teacher Tsong-Kha-pa (1357–1419). He built the great monasteries of Ganden, Drepung, and Sera for his followers. In their prime, these monasteries were like small cities, housing tens of thousands of monks. In the sixteenth century, the leader of the Gelukpas was given the title Dalai Lama by the Mongols. The title means "ocean of wisdom," meaning someone whose wisdom is as deep as the ocean.

This map shows the major Buddhist temples and monasteries of Tibet.

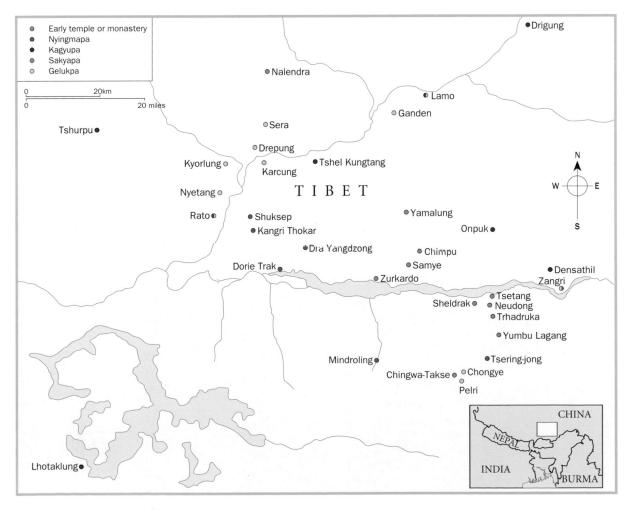

The Dalai Lamas The title of Dalai Lama was given to Sonam Gyatso (1543–88), but he accorded the honor to two previous Gelukpa leaders. Consequently, Gedun Truppa (1391–1475) is considered the first Dalai Lama. The current Dalai Lama is the fourteenth. Tibetans believe that the Dalai Lama is the incarnation of the bodhisattva, Avalokitesvara, who deliberately chose to be reborn in human form in order to help other suffering beings. When a Dalai Lama dies, a search is conducted for a baby who is the next incarnation. He is identified by various signs; for example, he may be able to recognize old friends from his previous incarnation or pick out belongings such as prayer beads. The baby is taken from his family and spends many years being educated in Lhasa, the Tibetan capital.

By the seventeenth century, the fifth Dalai Lama (1617–82) had become the religious and political leader of Tibet. He built the famous Potala Palace in Lhasa. Over the following centuries, the Dalai Lamas were caught up in political intrigue, particularly over Chinese claims to Tibet. During this time, the Dalai Lamas were forced to give up some political power to the Chinese. This remained the situation until the thirteenth Dalai Lama (1875–1933) assumed full power and ruled Tibet until his death.

Chinese invasion

In 1951, Chinese Communist forces invaded Tibet. At first, efforts were made to combine Communism with Buddhist religious freedom. But Communists objected to many Buddhist practices, and most Tibetans objected to Chinese rule. Thousands of monks were imprisoned or killed, and Buddhist teachings were outlawed. In 1959, after an unsuccessful Tibetan uprising, the fourteenth Dalai Lama was forced to flee in disguise from Lhasa. He settled in India where he was joined by approximately 100,000 fellow Tibetans. Those left behind suffered terribly. Persecution in Tibet became worse during the Chinese

THE FOURTEENTH DALAI LAMA

The current Dalai Lama, Tenzin Gyatso, is the fourteenth incarnation of the bodhisattva. He was born in 1935, taken to Lhasa at the age of five and made the head of state at sixteen. From his home in India, the Dalai Lama travels all over the world, campaigning for the rights of the Tibetan people. His warmth, wisdom, and compassion have made him a much-loved and respected statesman. In 1989, he was awarded the Nobel Peace Prize for his work.

Tenzin Gyatso, the fourteenth Dalai Lama, at his home in Dharamsala, India.

Cultural Revolution of the 1960s. Buddhist temples and works of art were systematically destroyed, and the great monasteries were reduced to ghost towns. In 20 years, a centuries-old way of life had been devastated.

Tibetan Buddhism in exile

Today, the Dalai Lama and his many Buddhist monks are still based in Dharamsala, India, where they have established a thriving Tibetan community and government in exile. The town has several Buddhist monasteries and temples, a school of Tibetan studies, and workshops where traditional works of Tibetan Buddhist art are produced. Since 1980, the Chinese rulers have granted some limited religious freedom in Tibet, but the Dalai Lama has not been allowed to return, and Buddhism in Tibet faces a very uncertain future.

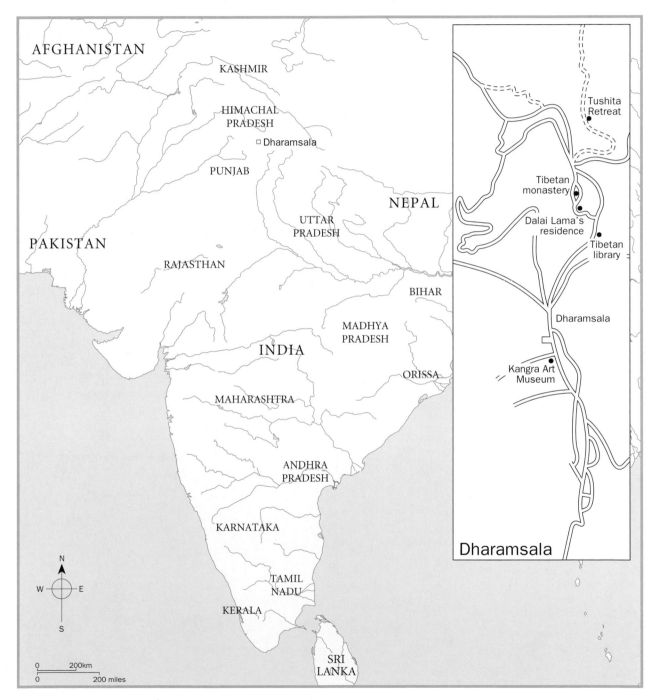

This map shows the location of Dharamsala, India, where the current Dalai Lama has lived in exile since 1959.

CHAPTER 6:
BUDDHISM IN THE MODERN WORLD

Buddhism confronts many challenges as it moves into the twenty-first century. In Buddhism's Asian homeland, the twentieth century proved a time of mixed fortunes. In some countries, Buddhists faced persecution under brutal governments. In others, war and national unrest threatened Buddhism. However, Buddhism has recently begun to reestablish itself in countries such as India and Indonesia. It is also gaining new followers in non-Asian countries, especially in Europe, North America, and Australia.

Buddhism and society In Asian countries such as Thailand and Sri Lanka, Buddhism is still the main religion and has a strong influence on society. For centuries, the sangha has played a vital role. Monks are involved in education, health and social work, and in conservation. They continue to act as spiritual advisors to local communities, helping people live according to Buddhist principles. In return, they are treated with great respect by the local people, as they have for hundreds of years.

Engaged Buddhism Today, many Buddhists in Asia and beyond are becoming involved in "engaged Buddhism." This means engaging in many aspects of social work, peace activism, politics, and human rights. For example, Buddhists have established hospitals and AIDS charities, visited prisons, and led protests against global concerns such as the international arms trade. One famous example of engaged Buddhism is the Wat Tham Krabok monastery in Thailand. For the last 50 years, the monks and nuns at this monastery have administered a strict but successful detoxification program for drug addicts, based on Buddhist principles.

Buddhist monks protest against an alcohol company in Bangkok, Thailand.

BUDDHISM IN INDIA

Today, Hinduism and Islam are the major religions in India, though Buddhism has shown signs of revival. This is largely due to the work of Dr. B. R. Ambedkar (1891–1956), an Indian lawyer and politician. He was born into a Dalit family, the lowest rank of Indian Hindu society. Hostility against his campaigns for equal rights for Dalits led Ambedkar to convert to Buddhism. Millions of other Dalits followed his example.

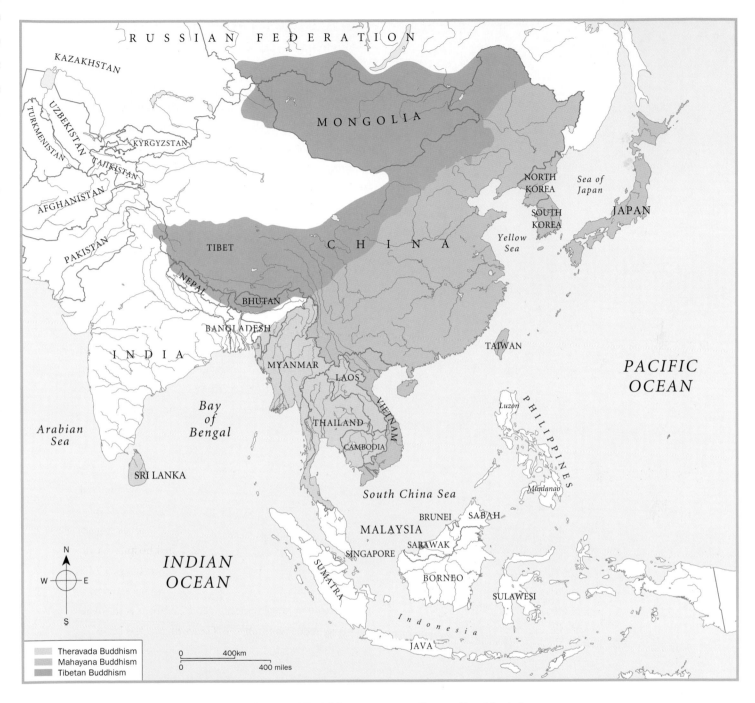

This map shows where different forms of Buddhism are currently practiced in Asia.

Buddhism and politics

In many Asian countries, Buddhism has suffered greatly under Communist and military regimes. Vietnam has been under Communist rule since the 1950s. Buddhism has survived alongside Communism, but the sangha is regulated by the government. However, in Cambodia, Buddhism was practically wiped out. From 1975 to 1979, a Communist movement called the Khmer Rouge held power. Under its leader, Pol Pot, many monasteries were destroyed, and thousands of monks were tortured and killed. In 1979, a delegation of monks had to be sent from Vietnam to revive Cambodia's sangha. Today, Buddhism is officially the state religion of Cambodia, but its recovery has been slow and its future is unknown.

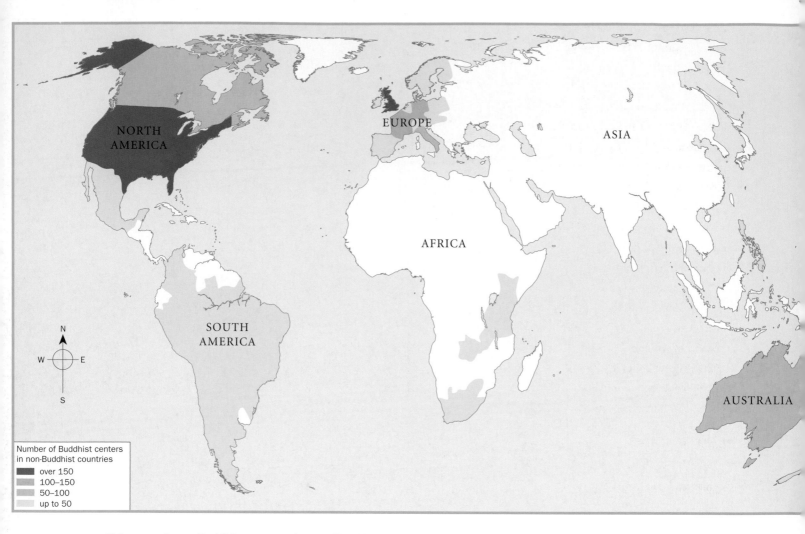

This map shows Buddhist centers in non-Buddhist countries outside Asia.

Number of Buddhist centers
in non-Buddhist countries

- over 150
- 100–150
- 50–100
- up to 50

Buddhism in the West

Until about 100 years ago, few people in the West had heard of Buddhism. But over the last century, there has been greater contact between Buddhism and the West. Buddhism has grown rapidly and attracted thousands of followers. It has now become firmly established in the United States, the United Kingdom, Australia, and in most European countries. It is also becoming more popular in South America and Africa.

Buddhist scholars

The British encountered Buddhism in the late eighteenth and early nineteenth centuries, when the British Empire expanded to include Buddhist countries such as Burma and Ceylon. Some of the first Westerners to study Buddhism were British civil servants working in these countries. Other Buddhist countries, such as Vietnam and Cambodia, came under French colonial rule, and French scholars also studied Buddhism.

In 1879, Edward Arnold, a British teacher in India, published a poem called "The Light of Asia," based on the Buddha's life. This helped spread an awareness of the Buddha; serious scholarship began in the UK when the Pali Text Society was founded in 1881 by British scholar T. W. Rhys Davids (1843–1922). He first came across Buddhism while working for the British civil service in Ceylon. The society collected Theravada Buddhist texts and translated them, making Buddhism accessible to people in the West.

Buddhist societies

At the beginning of the twentieth century, the first Westerners became Buddhist monks. Among them was a British man, Alan Bennett (1873–1923). Bennett was ordained in Burma and took the Buddhist name Ananda Maitreya. In 1908, he helped establish the first Buddhist society in the UK. In 1926, Anagarika Dharmapala (1874–1933) established a Buddhist center in London, the first outside Asia. Buddhist societies were also formed in Germany, in 1903 and 1924, and France, in 1929. The Buddhist Society of America was formed in 1930, in New York City.

Since then, interest in Buddhism has grown rapidly, and new centers and societies open every year. There are currently more than 1,800 centers in the U.S. Some are mainly for people who have emigrated from Asia; others cater to Westerners who want to learn meditation or follow a Buddhist way of life. There are also many Buddhist monasteries in the Western world, run by Western monks and nuns.

THE THEOSOPHICAL SOCIETY

An organization called the Theosophical Society helped introduce Buddhist ideas to the West. Founded in 1875 in New York by two Americans, Colonel Henry Steel Olcott (1832–1907) and Helena Blavatsky (1831–91), the Society drew its ideas from different religious traditions, including Hinduism and Buddhism. Olcott and Blavatsky may have been the first Westerners to formally become Buddhists. On a visit to Ceylon in 1880, they visited a temple and pledged themselves to Buddhism in the presence of a Buddhist monk.

Madame Helena Petrovna Blavatsky (1831–91).

Western Buddhists take part in a Tibetan Buddhist ceremony in Dharamsala.

Buddhist traditions in the West

Before the 1950s, Theravada was the form of Buddhism that was well-known in the West. Then, in 1954, a Ceylonese vihara—a Buddhist temple—was established in London, followed by a Thai vihara in 1966. In the mid-1950s, Japanese Zen Buddhism also became popular in the U.S. and the UK. In the 1960s and 1970s, Tibetan refugees set up centers in the U.S., the UK, Europe, and Australia. A Tibetan monk named Chogyam Trungpa established the Samye Ling Monastery in Scotland and a Tibetan Buddhist center in the U.S. Today, it is estimated that about half of Western Buddhists follow a form of Tibetan Buddhism. Other smaller groups have also become well established, such as Japanese Pure Land and Shingon. Modern Buddhist groups have also developed, including Soka-gakkai, a branch of Nichiren Buddhism. Its teachings are based on daily chanting as a means not only to spiritual, but also material, rewards. Many Buddhists have criticized this approach.

New Kadampa movement One of the fastest-growing Buddhist groups in the West is the New Kadampa tradition. Founded by the Tibetan monk Geshe Kelsang Gyatso Rinpoche, it has over 900 meditation centers in 37 countries. New Kadampa is based on Kadampa Buddhism, which dates back to eleventh-century Tibet. It emphasizes moral discipline, study, and meditation as ways to peace and happiness. Followers of New Kadampa also worship a spirit called Dorje Shugden. In 1998, the first New Kadampa temple was built in the UK. A second temple is nearly finished in New York City, and more temples are planned.

FRIENDS OF THE WESTERN BUDDHIST ORDER

The Friends of the Western Buddhist Order (FWBO) was started in 1967 by a British Buddhist monk named Venerable Sangharakshita (born Dennis Lingwood). During World War II, he was stationed in India and present-day Sri Lanka. He remained in Asia after the war and was ordained as a Theravada monk. He also studied the teachings of Tibetan and Chan Buddhism. He decided to form a Buddhist movement that combined elements of traditional Buddhism in a way that was accessible to Western society. For example, the FWBO does not have monks and nuns. Committed Buddhists take serious vows and are ordained as "members." They do not wear robes but have a scarf, called a *kesa*, for special ceremonies.

Future of Buddhism In some traditionally Buddhist countries, such as Thailand and Sri Lanka, the primary values and teachings of Buddhism—tolerance, compassion, and morality—have been undermined by a growing concern with material wealth. In other places, where Buddhism has arrived more recently, it is precisely these values that have attracted new followers. Even for people who are not religious, Buddhist ideas and practices, such as meditation, have been influential. But what is the future of Buddhism? A key Buddhist teaching states that nothing stays the same forever; the world is always changing. By adapting to different cultures and circumstances, Buddhism has established itself as a major world faith that should continue to thrive.

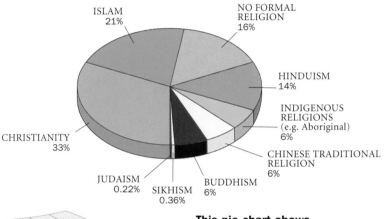

This pie chart shows the size of the world's Buddhist population compared to other faiths.

This map shows the places where different faiths are in the majority.

Buddhism
Christianity
Hinduism
Indigenous Religions
Islam
Judaism
Nonreligious
Sikhism

GREAT LIVES

Siddhartha Gautama (ca. 563–483 BCE)

Siddhartha Gautama, who became the Buddha, was the son of an Indian nobleman. Siddhartha was born in Lumbini, Nepal, and his sheltered, early life was spent in his father's luxurious palace. When he saw people suffer for the first time, he left palace life to live as a monk, searching for life's truth. Having achieved enlightenment, he realized what caused suffering and spent the rest of his life teaching ways to end suffering and to live a better life.

Ashoka (ruled ca. 265–238 BCE)

Ashoka was an Indian ruler of the Mauryan Empire who converted to Buddhism. To promote Buddhist teachings, he had edicts carved on rocks and pillars that were placed around his empire. He also sent many missionaries, including his own son and daughter, to spread the Buddha's teachings beyond India.

Asvaghosa (first century CE)

Asvaghosa was a poet at the court of the Kushan king Kanishka. He wrote many works on Buddhism in Sanskrit, including the first biography of the Buddha, entitled the *Buddhacarita* (*Acts of the Buddha*). Written in the style of an epic poem, parts of the original work still survive. There are also Tibetan and Chinese translations.

Nagarjuna (150–ca. 250)

Nagarjuna was the founder of the Madhyamika school of Buddhism and the greatest Buddhist philosopher. He was born into a Hindu family but became a Buddhist as a young man. It is said that he was presented with a collection of sacred texts by the king of the Nagas, who were mythical serpents with magical powers.

Bodhidharma (ca. fifth century)

Bodhidharma was an Indian monk who traveled to China and became the founder of Chan (Zen) Buddhism. It is said that he spent nine years sitting still and meditating, then taught this method of meditation to his followers. According to tradition, he decided to return to India but died before he could do so.

Atisha (982–1054)

Atisha was an Indian monk and teacher who strongly influenced the development of Buddhism in Tibet. He is said to have studied Buddhism in Indonesia before becoming abbot of the Buddhist university of Vikramasila in India. In 1024, he was invited to Tibet by the king, where he guided the monks on the Buddha's teachings.

Dogen (1200–53)

Dogen was the founder of the Soto Zen school in Japan and a major figure in Japanese Buddhism. Dogen was born into an aristocratic family, but his father died when he was three and his mother when he was eight. At the age of 13, he entered the great Tendai monastery at Mount Hiei. He devoted the rest of his life to training his followers in the teachings and practices of Zen.

Nichiren (1222–82)

Nichiren was a Japanese monk who founded the Nichiren school of Buddhism. The son of a fisherman, he joined a Tendai monastery at the age of 12. For many years, he traveled from temple to temple, searching for the teachings of "true Buddhism." He was exiled for his outspoken beliefs and narrowly avoided execution.

Thich Nhat Hanh (born 1926)

Thich Nhat Hanh is a Vietnamese Zen master who was ordained at the age of 16. In the 1960s, during the Vietnam War, he worked hard to help war-torn communities and to campaign for peace. He continued his work after leaving Vietnam and founded Plum Village in France, where people from different faiths can attend retreats.

Tenzin Gyatso (born 1935)

The current Dalai Lama was born in northeastern Tibet. When he was five, he was taken to Lhasa and installed on the throne. At the age of 16, he became the head of state. In 1959, the Dalai Lama was forced to flee to Dharamsala, India, with many of his monks. He continued to travel and work tirelessly on behalf of the Tibetan people. He was awarded the Nobel Peace Prize in 1989.

FACTS AND FIGURES

Approximate number of Buddhists worldwide, by tradition (2004)

Mahayana	56%	185,000,000
Theravada	38%	124,000,000
Tibetan	6%	20,000,000

Countries with the highest percentages of Buddhists (2004)

Thailand	95%
Cambodia	90%
Myanmar	88%
Bhutan	75%
Sri Lanka	70%
Tibet	65%
Laos	60%
Vietnam	55%
Japan	50%
Macau	45%
Taiwan	43%

Countries with the largest Buddhist populations (2004)

China	102,000,000
Thailand	55,480,000
Vietnam	49,690,000
Myanmar	41,610,000
Sri Lanka	12,540,000
South Korea	10,920,000
Taiwan	9,150,000
Cambodia	9,130,000
Japan	8,965,000

Source: Buddha Dharma Education Association and BuddhaNet

Calendar of festivals

Month of festival	Event	What happens
April	Hana-Matsuri (Japanese Mahayana)	A flower festival celebrating the Buddha's birthday and the coming of spring in Japan.
April/May	Wesak (Theravada)	Special prayers are said and gifts are exchanged to celebrate the Buddha's birthday, enlightenment, and passing.
June/July	Chokhor (Vajrayana)	A Tibetan and Nepalese summer festival observing the Buddha's first teaching of the Four Noble Truths.
June/July	Poson (Theravada)	A Sri Lankan festival celebrating the arrival of Buddhism on the island with huge street parades telling the story.
July/August	O-bon (Japanese Mahayana)	A time for remembering people who have died, celebrated with feasts and folk dances.
July/August	Asala (Theravada)	A festival observed in Kandy, Sri Lanka, with a spectacular parade in which an elephant carries a sacred relic of a tooth that is believed to have been the Buddha's.
August	Festival of Hungry Ghosts (Chinese Mahayana)	A time for remembering the story of one of the Buddha's followers who saved his mother from hell by offering a feast to all the monks.
October/November	Kathina (Theravada)	A time when lay Buddhists visit the temple to give gifts of new robes to the monks.
November	Loi Kratong (Theravada)	The festival of lights in Thailand, when people float lighted candles in the rivers and remember the Buddha's generosity and kindness.
November	Sangha Day (FWBO)	A festival that celebrates the love and friendship shared by the sangha. A special prayer is said, and people renew their commitment to Buddhism.
February	Losar (Vajrayana)	The Tibetan New Year festival, when the prayer flags fluttering from the temples are taken down and replaced.

TIME LINE

ca. 563	Siddhartha Gautama is born in Lumbini, Nepal.
ca. 483	The Buddha dies in Kushinagara, India.
ca. 482	The First Council is held at Rajagrha.
ca. 373	The Second Council is held at Vesali.
326	The armies of Alexander the Great reach India.
265–232	Reign of Emperor Ashoka.
ca. 250	Buddhism is introduced in Ceylon (Sri Lanka).
250	The Third Council is held at Pataliputra.
155–130	Reign of King Milinda (Menandros).
first century	The Tripitaka is written down for the first time.

CE

first century	The first images of the Buddha are made in Gandhara; Buddhism reaches China and is established in Indonesia.
100	The Fourth Council is held in Kashmir.
fourth century	Buddhism probably reaches Korea.
fifth century	The University of Nalanda is at its height; Buddhism becomes established in Burma (Myanmar).
sixth century	Buddhism is established in Vietnam; Buddhism reaches Japan from Korea.
seventh century	Buddhism is introduced in Tibet.
ca. 800	Borobudur is built on the island of Java.
twelfth century	Buddhism becomes the religion of Cambodia; Buddhism almost disappears from India; Nalanda is destroyed by the Muslims.
1350	Buddhism becomes the religion of Thailand.
1391–1475	The first Dalai Lama in Tibet.
1881	The Pali Text Society is founded.
1908	The first Buddhist Society in the UK.
1930	The first Buddhist Society in the U.S.
1935	Birth of the fourteenth Dalai Lama.
1956	In India, Dr. Ambedkar converts many people to Buddhism just before his death.
1959	The Dalai Lama flees Tibet.
1967	The Friends of the Western Buddhist Order is founded.
1989	The Dalai Lama wins the Nobel Peace Prize.

GLOSSARY

alms Charitable donations of food and other items to Buddhist monks and nuns.

arhats Theravada Buddhists who have gained enlightenment and are treated with great respect and reverence.

bo tree The fig tree under which the Buddha is said to have gained enlightenment.

bodhisattvas In Mahayana Buddhism, mythical beings who have gained enlightenment and could become Buddhas, but choose to help other people overcome suffering.

Bon The ancient religion of Tibet, before Buddhism arrived. It involves the worship of many spirits, gods, and demons. Bon priests use magic and sacrifices to keep the spirits happy.

Buddhism The religion based on the teachings of Siddhartha Gautama, who became the Buddha. These teachings are known as the dharma.

Communist A system of government in which the state owns industries and businesses and establishes a classless society.

Confucianism An ancient Chinese religion founded by Confucius in the sixth century BCE. It teaches respect for other people and believes in honoring the memory of ancestors.

cremated When a dead body is burned to ashes.

dowry Goods or a sum of money, traditionally given to an Indian bridegroom's family by a bride's family before a marriage.

edicts Proclamations by a king or other authority.

enlightenment Achieving a state of spiritual understanding.

Hinduism The ancient religion of India that began more than 4,000 years ago. Today, it is India's major religion with approximately 800 million followers.

incarnation An appearance of a god or god-like being in human form. For example, Tibetans believe that the Dalai Lama is an incarnation of the bodhisattva Avalokitesvara.

Islam A religion that began in the Middle East in the seventh century CE, based on the teachings of the Prophet Muhammad.

laypersons People who follow a religion but have not become monks or nuns.

Mahayana One of the two main branches of Buddhism. Mahayana means "the great way."

meditate To quiet the mind in order to experience inner peace. Meditation is a central part of Buddhist practice.

missionaries People who travel in order to teach others about a religion and convert them to that faith.

Muslims Followers of the religion of Islam.

nationalism Great loyalty or devotion to one's country.

nirvana The state of perfect peace and happiness that is entered when the cycle of birth and rebirth is broken and suffering ends.

ordained Describes a person who has undergone a special ceremony to become a monk, nun, or other member of a religious order.

patron A person who gives support to a particular cause.

pilgrimages Journeys made to places that are sacred.

relics Parts of a holy person's body or belongings, retained after his or her death as an object of reverence.

sangha The community of Buddhists. For some Buddhists, the sangha particularly means monks and nuns; for others, it includes laypersons as well.

Sanskrit An ancient Indian language used to write down many of the Mahayana sacred texts. It is also the sacred language of Hinduism.

Shinto The ancient religion of Japan. Its followers believe in spirits called *kami*, which live in animals, plants, and natural places such as rivers and mountains.

stupas Dome-shaped Buddhist monuments originally built to house the Buddha's relics.

Taoism An ancient Chinese religion founded by Lao-tzu in the sixth century BCE. It teaches the Tao, or "Way," the spiritual force of the universe.

Theravada One of the two main branches of Buddhism. Theravada means "the way of the elders."

Tripitaka The sacred texts of the Theravada Buddhists.

vihara A Buddhist monastery or temple.

FURTHER INFORMATION

Books for younger readers

DK Eyewitness Guides: Buddhism by Philip Wilkinson (Dorling Kindersley, 2003)

Puja: The FWBO Book of Buddhist Devotional Texts by Adiccabandhu and Padmasri (Windhorse Publications, 2004)

World of Beliefs: Buddhism by Anita Ganeri (New Line Books, 2006)

Books for older readers

Buddha by Karen Armstrong (Penguin Books, 2004)

Buddhism: A History by Noble Ross Reat (Jain Publishing, 1996)

Buddhism for Beginners by Thubten Chodron (Snow Lion Publications, 2001)

Web sites

www.buddhanet.net
A Buddhist network giving information on a wide range of Buddhist topics.

www.fwbo.org
The official Web site of the Friends of the Western Buddhist Order.

www.newyorkbuddhist.org
The Web site of the New York Theravada vihara.

www.tibet.com
The official Web site of the Tibetan government in exile, with information about Tibetan Buddhism, language, and art.

INDEX